# SCHIRMER'S LIBRARY OF MUSICAL CLASSICS

Vol. 1574

JOHANN SEBASTIAN BACH

Two- and Three-Part Inventions

For the Piano

Edited by

FERRUCCIO BUSONI

English Translations by

FREDERICK H. MARTENS and DR. THEODORE BAKER

ISBN 978-0-7935-4994-8

G. SCHIRMER, Inc.

DISTRIBUTED BY

HAL•LEONARD
CORPORATION

7777 W. BLUEMOUND RD. P.O. BOX 13819 MILWAUKEE, WI 53213

Printed in the U.S.A. by G. Schirmer, Inc.

PREFACE TO THE FIRST EDITION

Close scrutiny of the average system of musical instruction now in vogue has convinced me that Bach's Inventions are, in most cases, used only as a dry, technical training material for beginners in piano-playing, and that piano-teachers do little or nothing to awaken in their pupils an understanding for the profounder significance of these compositions.

The study of the Inventions is limited, in general, to a wholly unsystematic selection from among them; the frequent employment of faulty or poorly edited editions provided with unreliable expression-marks and embellishment-signs, makes it only the harder for the student to enter into the spirit of Bach; lastly, the important feature of structural analysis is in most cases entirely omitted from the instruction, although it is calculated, more than any other means, to develop the student's musicianship and sharpen his critical insight.

When a mind of so broad a scope as Bach's voices an intention to show, in these pieces, "a plain way" in order "to gain withal a keen foretaste of composition," we may assume that the Master followed a well-considered plan in his work, and that in each and every combination therein occurring there lies a secret and a significance.

In preparing this revision it has been my aim to make this significance clearer to the general comprehension.

Moscow, 1891.   FERRUCCIO BUSONI.

Attention is called to the details of chief importance in this edition:

(1) A perfectly clear presentation of the musical text throughout. (Notably as regards correctness, the execution of embellishments, and the allocation of the middle part in the three-part movements.)

(2) Choice of suitable fingering. (Notably as to use of the thumb and the 5th finger on black keys; the succession of fingers in diatonic figures with thumb held down: (a) Ascending with 3 4 3—4 5 4—4 5 3 4—4 5 2 3, etc. (b) Descending with 5 4 5—4 3 4 4 3 5 4—3 2 5 4, etc. (c) Employing the "parallel" fingers 1 3—2 4—3 5 3 1—4 2—5 3 in diatonic progressions and trills. (d) Avoiding change of fingers on a held note.

(3) Indication of the tempo. N.B. The Italian and English phrases are not intended to be mutual translations, but rather to supplement each other; the Italian tempo-marks being often stiff and conventional, and so not giving the finer shades of meaning, whereas the English do not always adequately render certain established conceptions (e.g., Andante, Allegro).

(4) The expression-marks, intended to serve as a guide to a correct conception of Bach's style.—This style is characterized, above all, by virility, energy, breadth and grandeur. Sentimental nuances, use of the pedal, the *arpeggiando, tempo rubato,* even an all too smooth *legato* and too frequent *piano,* are to be avoided, in general, as oppugnant to the character of Bach.

(5) The foot-notes, which—alongside of the suggestions for pianistic technique, and remarks on the interpretation—are intended chiefly as aids in the teaching of formal construction.

PREFACE TO THE SECOND EDITION

On looking over this work, done more than twenty years ago, it impresses me as logically complete as it stands, and so I have concluded, despite many changes in my views, to reprint it *without alteration*.

The student is warned against following my "interpretations" too literally. Here the moment and the individual have rights peculiarly their own. My conception may serve as a trustworthy guidepost, to which no one need give heed who knows some other good way.

True, for most of the Inventions there is probably only the one way; with regard to some, my own feeling has undergone a change.

For example, I now find it in better taste to play the theme of No. 8 under *one continuous legato-slur;* I should now *tone down* the accents of No. 11, and phrase the last one as follows:

At present I employ very little, or not at all, the change of fingers on repeated notes (likewise in mordents and inverted mordents), and am more and more given to avoid the passing-under of the thumb.

Finally, I no longer dwell on petty details and subordinate issues; I lay more stress on the expression of a face than on the cut of its features.

Berlin, July, 1914.   FERRUCCIO BUSONI.

To the Music Institute in Helsingfors,
The Editor

Fifteen Two-Part Inventions

Edited by F. B. Busoni

English version by
Frederick H. Martens

Johann Sebastian Bach

Allegro
With animation and decision

(1) That a ♯ preceded the C on the second eighth-note of the measure is almost invariably forgotten by the pupil. Experience has dictated the advisability of repeating the ♯ before the second C♯ to be played.

(1a) In order to avoid the collision of both thumbs on the same key, the place of the bracketed E in the left hand may be taken by a sixteenth-rest.

(2) The same as at (1).

(3) The establishment of the principal key is sufficiently pronounced in the second measure before the last to make superfluous any holding back in the tempo of the measure before the last, where the imminence of the following close is clearly expressed.

(4) The inexplicable *arpeggiando*-sign, which accompanies this final chord in numerous editions, is in absolute contradiction to the virile style of the composition, and so far as regards Bach, must be termed a stylistic error. We wish to warn students, in particular, against effeminization of this kind, here and in analogous places.

N. B. With regard to the *form* of this piece, it is in the main so arranged that it may be called a *three-part* invention. The half-measure theme: (the bracketed eighth-note is treated freely, as an interval) underlies the entire composition; the closing formulas alone, which invariably terminate one of the three sections (indicated by double-bars *), testify to the non-employ of the principal theme. The theme first appears four times in alternation in the upper and lower parts, and then, in a quadruple sequence of its *inversion*, carries out a downward progression in the upper part; which progression at the same time accomplishes the modulation to the dominant key. In the fifth measure the sequential extension of the second half of the theme finally leads to the dominant cadence on which the first section ends. The second section (cadencing in the relative key) is almost entirely symmetrical in relation to the first, in which both parts exchange rôles. The intercalated third and fourth measures — a free, symmetrical imitation of the two preceding ones — have chiefly a modulatory significance. This duplication of the two initial measures in section two assumes organic shape in the *third* section, where the theme, alternating by measures, appears in its original form as well as in contrary motion. Worthy of notice, in this instance, is this transformation of the eighth-note movement, hitherto used, of the "counter-phrase" (the counterpoint led over the theme) into a tied half-note; and the subsequent inversion of the originally descending, but now (by a triple interlocking of the type theme) *ascending* movement, which triumphantly leads back into the principal key.

Incisive, rhythmic playing will most adequately express this model worklet.

---

* Double-bars have been used in each of the 30 Inventions to indicate the close of the individual sections.

Moderato
Expressively, but not dragging

2

dolce, semplice

(1) **N.C.** = new counterpoint, must be regarded in this instance only as a harmonic necessity, to make the transition to the dominant more evident. In accordance with the general basic conception of the form here presented the **A** in the lower voice might otherwise appear *uncovered* while the upper voice rests.

(2) Actually and originally the second eighth once appears as follows:

(3) For technical reasons which are self-evident the inverted mordent on D has been omitted.

(4) F.C. = free close.

N.B. The entirely novel imprint given this invention — compared with its predecessor — in form, character and content, makes a corresponding difference in presentation essential. Before all else, in this invention, it is the *canonical* aspect, usually overlooked, which must be clearly and comprehensively revealed, and on the correct presentation of which recognition of its form depends.

The two-measure phrase (A) which takes the place of the theme at the beginning is repeated in the third and fourth measures of the second part in the lower octave, whereas the part progresses contrapuntally (B) above it. This counterpoint (B), in turn, is treated in the same manner in the lower part, and a *new* counterpoint (C) is built up upon it. Thus, in succession — two measures at a time — D is placed above C, E above D. The upper part, in consequence, takes shape as an uninterrupted, continuous ten-measure movement, developed by the linking of A, B, C, D and E, which, two measures later, also sounds in the lower part. Since both parts, however, conclude their imitative course with the tenth measure at the same time, the phrase E has to be dropped in the imitating part. On the other hand, the lower part sets in *first* in the second section, and the entire sequence is repeated in the subdominant key and in an inversion of the double counterpoint for another ten measures.

* The two measures which now follow serve to effect the modulatory return to the tonic, and, so to say, stand on neutral ground, *between* Section II and the abruptly closing Section III.
87640

Vivace, quasi allegro
Vivaciously and forcefully

3

(1) Although this measure unquestionably must be regarded as forming part of the *theme*, the figure: nevertheless, is of slight significance because — save in the analogous case in Section III — it only appears *once* more in the course of the composition and then at 1ᵃ.

(2) At a more rapid tempo — the interpretation admits of various shadings in the movement of tonal groups — the editor would advise that the passage be simplified, as follows: . The rhythmic and melodic outlines never should sound blurred.

(3) The thematic progression by seconds takes a leap of a third at +.

(4) In the working-out, three sixteenth-notes are placed before the two up-beat sixteenth-notes of the theme, whereby the following figure results: . This version is also used in the Coda.

N. B. With the same strictness observed in exactly holding down the key in the case of sustained tones, the importance of the *rest,* on the other hand, also should be taken into account, by a corresponding raising of the hands.   The unoccupied hand (i. e., the *left*) is inclined to remain on the key, a habit which frequently results in the creation of unintentional organ-points, and hence should be suppressed at the very start.   This observation applies to similar places in all the Inventions and is of importance with regard to their *interpretation.*

---

* +−+ Actually: transitional measures from the second to the third sections (see note, ***** to preceding invention).

4

Allegro deciso
Quickly and forcefully

Ossia

(1) The "staccato" here called for should approximate on the piano the effect produced on the violin by the use of the "thrust" bowing. The prescribed time-value of the note should be mulcted only to the extent required to carry out a short, energetic movement of the wrist, before striking the following key.

(2) In order correctly to visualize the thematic structure, it is advisable to think of this figure as paralleling the beginning of Section II; somewhat as follows:

etc.

(3) The above trill with minor second, in Bach's sense, is entirely correct and in style, even though the "crossrelationship" to the upper part arising from it may give offence to hyperpuritanical musical ears. The trill in reality takes the place of the descending melodic minor scale; the theme concatenation moving above it the same scale ascending.

(4) The measure here intercalated, symmetrically akin to the close of the first section, already forecasts the end of the piece, so that one is inclined to consider the four measures which still succeed it as a Coda.

Allegro risoluto
Rapidly, forcefully and passionately

(1) The principal figure of the theme must be "hammered out," so to say, in the sturdiest *non legato*. The manner of execution here indicated will give an approximate portrayal of the character of this interpretation.

(2) The sixteenth-note figures of the counter theme, on the other hand, should flow along in the most equalized *legato*. The three figures which relieve each other have a tendency to confuse, at first, because of their similarity. Hence the player will do well to reduce them to rule by a comparison of their recurrence: This will notably aid his memory while, on the other hand, technical practice of the figure sequence will powerfully further finger control.

(3) The theme itself comprises four full measures, then undergoes an imitation in the dominant, and is finally used in fragmentary form for an ascending three-measure sequence. The second section corresponds in all ways to the first, with the sole exception that in it the sequence *descends* instead of ascending.

(4) The Editor regards the four measures which follow as the first half of the theme and its imitation in the tonic. Another, less justified conception would be: to connect the preceding last measure of Section II with the fourth measure of Section III (in a single sequence) and to regard all that lies between as an "extension."

(5) A broader *ritenuto* which, incidentally, seems quite in place, calls for an enrichment of the trill:

N. B. This number is the first of those two-part Inventions in which the countersubject plays an *obligato* rôle, those in which one and the same *counter theme* (counterpoint to the theme) is retained throughout the composition, and appears as the theme's inseparable companion. Numbers 6, 9, 11 and 12 also are inventions of this type. We have here called attention to this peculiarity once and for all.

Allegretto piacevole, quasi Andantino
With graceful movement, not rapidly

6

(1) This figure, in the Editor's opinion, should sound out in strict rhythm, not too *legato* and innocent of that modern elegance which, somehow, is not compatible with Bach's style. The alternative phrasing (in which, as a rule, the two thirty-second-notes are slightly hurried in tempo) therefore should be rejected.

(2) The *legato* in the upper part can be secured only by using the pedal as indicated.

(3) What has been said at (1) applies here in the fullest sense.

(4) The phrasing indicated is intended to suggest the *thematic* relation between this and the following parallel measures.

N. B. This invention, above all others, is the only one in which the end of the first section, in the original edition, is indicated by a double-bar. We have refrained from similarly marking Sections II and III at this point (indicated by the N. B.), in order not to cause confusion, in view of the fact that the repetition-mark at the close applies to *both sections together.*

The two-part song — it might be called an intermezzo for flute and violoncello in a pastoral cantata-captivates by reason of its gentle melodic charm, and the spontaneity of its contrapuntal movement; if various kinds of touch are employed in playing, it becomes a useful study for performance. It might be remarked, incidentally, that the third section is a contrapuntal inversion of the first, i. e., that save for a few variants which result from the continuation in the principal key, it represents a change of rôle on the part of the two voices.

Allegro moderato ma deciso
Quite lively and with decision

7*

* In view of its form and nature, this invention might be classed as a kind of *primary invention* which had attained a "high-er stage of development."

27640

Ossia

N. B. In contrapuntal movements the entrance of the organ-point on the dominant may always be accept-ed as a signal for the beginning of the *last section*. It is all the more so in this particular instance, since from this moment on the principal key is not again abandoned. The figure: and what follows should be regarded as a variant of and of its sequences.

Presto e leggero possible*
As rapidly and lightly as possible

(1) In all other editions this eighth-note appears tied over to the following sixteenth-note; yet this is in quite evident contradiction to the "up-beat" character of both figures, which clearly are separated one from the other.

(2) This measure and the one following (in the left hand), should be practised assiduously.

* That is to say in so far as is compatible with clarity.

N. B. Essentially this is a tripart form which, however, (analogous to Invention 2), gains greater importance owing to the added canonic development. The canon, which in the beginning carries out the imitation strictly in the octave, at (a), because of harmonic considerations, leaps down to the ninth below and breaks off at (b). The (c) marks the beginning of the development (Section II), in which a livelier modulatory movement and the entrance of a relatively new figure (d), are noticeable. If, where Sections II and III meet (e), the three measures elided in order not to interrupt the movement in sixteenths were to be restored, according to the scheme of Section 1:

we would have, in Section III *an exact copy of the whole of Section I,* transposed to ifs lower dominant: in this way we obtain a clear general view of the fundamental plan of the form.

In addition to the light and rapid manner of playing already indicated, the performance of this "little virtuoso piece" demands the utmost precision.

Allegro non troppo, ma con spirito
Not too lively, yet with a swing

(1) With regard to the countersubject see the N. B. for Invention 5.

(2) This measure must be counted as still belonging to the *theme,* since it repeatedly appears in connection with the latter and also is worked out.

(3) The upward leap of the sixth has here been reversed in order not to remove the upper part from the medial position.

---

* The leaping eighth-notes should be vigorously struck by both hands and move in strict rhythm. With regard to the manner of performance the indication *non leggero* might well be applied. *Non leggero,* however, is quite far removed from *pesante* (heavily), just as a *non legato* by no means is synonomous with a *staccato.*

(4) Here the original:  has been changed for harmonic reason; these last are especially in evidence in the second measure.

(5) A single return of the theme, extended by a closing cadence, can not be regarded as an *individual section*. Hence the six closing measures at this point must either be considered part of Section II, or else must be regarded as an *adjunct*. Once evident relationship between the precedent measure (∗) and the second-last measure of the composition is recognized, one is tempted to look upon the four measures lying between as an addition interpolated merely to satisfy the feeling for symmetry.

(6) This seemingly new counterpoint is actually only a transparent variant of the first countersubject. The figure ♫ should sound out in a robust *non legato*.

Tempo di Giga. Vivacissimo e leggero
With great animation and a skipping touch

10

(1) With a consistently quiet wrist the finger should leave the key *before* striking the key following. This, in particular, should first be practised slowly and vigorously, somewhat in the following manner:

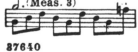

. These instructions, naturally, do not extend as well to the carrying out of the inverted mordents, which often are to be played *legato*, in which case only the three last notes (where they are not tied over) are to be struck *shortly*.

The carrying out of these instructions, after repeated playing of the composition, will result in a noticeable technical gain and will, in particular, further precision and lightness of touch.

(2) In order better to visualize the formal structure one should, as it were, imagine the entrance of a third, accessional part, the idea of which is approximately indicated in "reduced" form as follows:

(3) Pay attention to the analogy between this measure and the three measures following, and measures 2-5 of Section I.

(4) The leading of the upper part in this measure merely expresses the figuration of a suspension resting on the seventh, one which is resolved in the next measure: . In similar fashion, one measure later, the fundamental tone of the chord of the Dominant-Second (conceived as sustained) is embellished in the bass.

(5) This measure and the measure immediately following should be regarded merely as an "inner extension" of the movement, one which lends the melodic phrase, long drawn out, greater sweep and passion, and gives the final resolution, so to say, a certain stamp of "irrevocability." In a strictly organic sense the precedent measure is directly related to the second last measure of the composition; in which sense, it is true, the upper part must be thought of as occurring in the octave above.

N. B. The form is quite obviously a two-section one. With it all the two-part inventions which follow (with the exception of a few variants) also are in accord.

87640

Moderato espressivo (il tocco dolce, ma pieno)
Quietly movemented and expressive (with a soft yet full touch)

(1) The rôle assigned the countersubject (here wellnigh raised to the importance of an independent second theme) already has been explained in the N. B. to Invention No. 5.

(2) The fugal modulation to the dominant in this place is only *apparent,* inasmuch as the theme (aside from a little deviation of the interval of the seventh, marked +) actually is answered in the tonic.

(3) The reply of the countersubject takes place in the *contrary motion.* It begins half a measure later than the original, hence on the eighth eighth-note instead of the fourth eighth-note, and proceeds from the fifth. Because of its melodic and harmonic beauty it is a most admirable contrapuntal combination.

(4, 5) To be conceived as variants of the fundamental thematic idea are:

* Three-measure parallel passages at the end of Section 1 and Section 2, in the tonal relationship of dominant and tonic.

(6) In the wreathed line of this melodic figuration (to be played in a broadly expressive manner) the harmonic fundament may be recognized:

The player must strive to allow the *suspensional character* of the figuration, so to speak, "shine through".

N. B. 1. Owing to its equalized formal proprtions and its noble type of melody this invention must be accounted one of the most perfected models of its kind. It possesses a counterpart to correspond in the three-part Invention No. 7 (22).

N. B. 2. The eventual use of the embellishments in *small notes* is optional, in accordance with the player's taste.

24

Allegro vivace e brioso*
With great animation and sweep

12

f brillante Ossia

più leggero

f Ossia

più leggero

(2)

f

(sotto) (sopra) (sotto)

legg. *p*

p

(3)

f

più leggero

(1) At first, when playing slowly, the trill should be turned into a figure in thirty- second- notes:

At a very rapid tempo — and of this a really perfected performance admits — even the following would suffice:

(2) In accordance with the scale of the key of A major, in which we are moving, the mordent must choose the major second for its auxiliary note.

(3) The figure should be considered a variant of the theme:

* The pithy and robust "rolling off" of the figures and trills, while always observing the utmost clarity, makes per - missible a certain modern brilliancy, justified by the greater amplitude of the grand piano of our day. The virtuoso character of the composition, once technical infallibility is assured, even allows of a moderate employ of the pedal.

** See the N. B. to Invention No. 5.

(4) The *slurs* above the four succeeding appoggiature (each in the interval of a second — +), as a matter of fact, are traditional, yet not unimpugnable on this account. An uninterrupted staccato, in all probability, would be quite as valid.

(5) The Editor prefers to hasten energetically to the close, without any retarding of the tempo. Players who in this case find themselves at a loss without the time-honored Bachian "Allargando"— should they so prefer—may make use of the following ornament, to be found in the mss:

*** This case is similar to that mentioned in the note (5) to Invention No. 9.

Allegro giusto
Animated, the rhythm well marked

13

(1) In accordance with the precedent canonic scheme, it would be natural if at the two places here in question — instead of what follows — there were indicated a quarter-rest and a sixteenth-rest.

Of the four eighth-notes the *two first* notes should be somewhat more stressed, thereby allowing the imitative moment to come into its own.

(2) In many editions an A flat is incorrectly substituted for the A.

(3) The temptation to play the following: 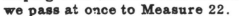 as a *two-part* passage — a possibility which is

quite explicable — should be resisted. The chordal figure of the "belated" quarter-note is *not* an ornamental concluding scroll; it is thematically grounded in the beginning of the third measure: and thereby its real meaning is made clear.

N. B. Apparently *division into two parts* is the predominating characteristic of this form, in accordance with which each of the two parts is again divided into two *sections*.

Yet an attempt to present the piece as *tripartite* may also be justified; it might take this shape, in particular, if we establish an imaginary connection between the first half of Measure 13 and the second half of Measure 17, and, consequently, regard what lies between as a transitional passage from Section II to Section III, thus:

In this conception each section represents a separate part.

The reading given in Friedemann Bach's "Klavierbüchlein" also permits only of a *tripartite* division. In the work in question, instead of Measures 16 and 17, we have the following variants of each and then, leaping over the next four measures, we pass at once to Measure 22.

Allegretto piacevole
Not too fast, with graceful and equalized movement

(1) The thematic *figure* is composed of two interlocking *up-beat* motives, one diatonic, the other chordal, whose interconnection may be considered as assuming somewhat the following shape:

The proof of the correctness of this conception is supplied, above all, by the development in Section II (+ — +), in which *only the first* of the two motives presented is worked out. The Editor finds it advisable to treat this First Motive as the variation of a *syncopation*, whereby the rhythmic accentuation here demanded may be secured with ease:

Inversion

It is from the triple interlocking of the figure already mentioned and from its inversion that the actual thematic *subject* results.

(2) The *answer* to the theme (thematic subject) in the dominant occurs only after a four measure (resp. two measure) interlude. At the same time, it forms the conclusion of Section I, representing a sixteen-measure period. Because of its rare simplicity this form, complete in itself, by all means deserves to be called the "primal form" of its type.

(3) In the original the time-value of the **D** is doubled.

N. B. 1. The original notation takes shape as follows:

With the doubling of the note-values the presentation of the text may be said to have gained with regard to lucidity and conciseness.

N. B. 2. What has been said in the note (5) to Inversion No. 9. also, with some slight modification, applies to what follows here. In this instance we have *eight measures* instead of six; the eight, however, in so far as form is concerned, correspond absolutely to the six of the other inversion.

Moderato ma con spirito
Easily, yet with spontaneous movement

(1) The theme embraces two full measures.

(2) A *whole close* instead of the original *half-close*, in the theme.

(3) Although this incidental canonic moment is, perhaps, unpremeditated, it should, nevertheless, not be allowed to pass unnoticed by the listener.

(4) This figure and the three figures following, each comprising two quarter-notes, are a free imitation of the precedent thematic fragment: . To secure greater smoothness of movement, the inverted mordent has been changed to a skip of a third. In the second measure the progression of a second, on the second eighth-note (+), is inverted and becomes a descending seventh.

(5) The *answer* in the tonic is here anticipated by one half-measure.

(6) The D should be regarded as the seventh of the secondary chord of the seventh on the fourth degree:

Appendix
Variant of Invention I

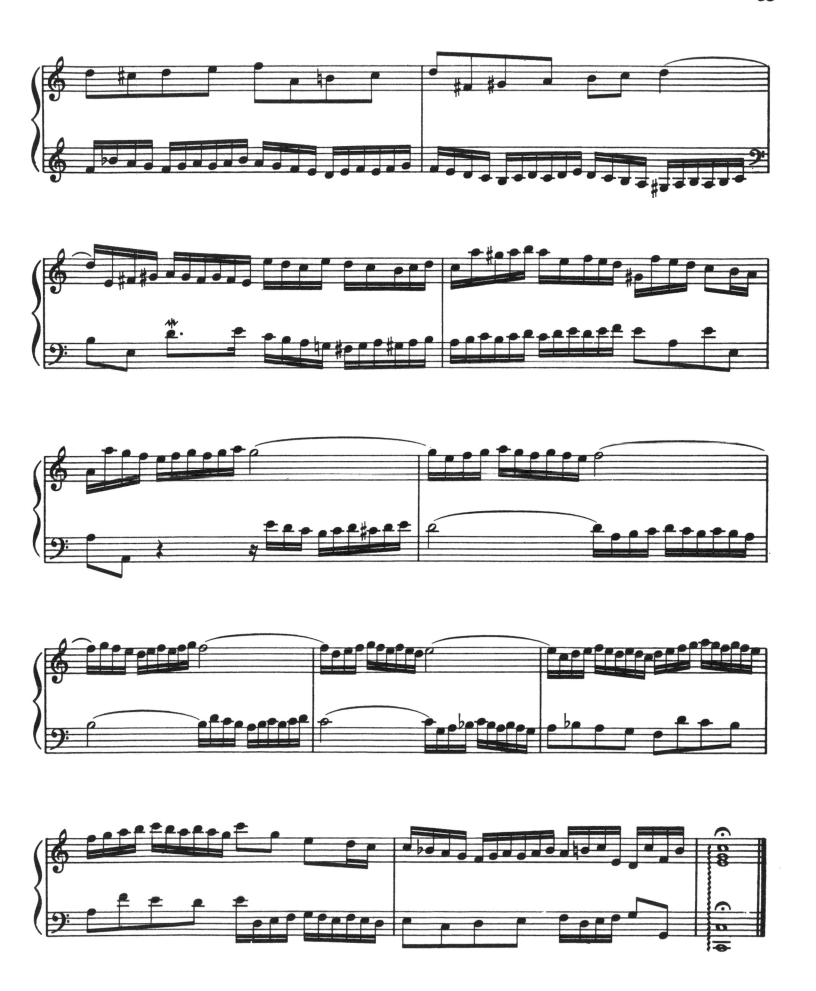

To the Music Institute in Helsingfors
The Editor

Fifteen Three-Part Inventions

English version by
Dr. Th. Baker

Johann Sebastian Bach
Edited by F. B. Busoni

Allegro deciso
Rapid and flowing

(1) To facilitate reading, bear in mind the following rule: Notes printed on the upper staff are to be played by the right hand, those on the lower staff, by the left hand.

(2) Inversion of theme (theme in contrary motion).

(3) A student confronted here for the first time by the problem of executing a three-part contrapuntal movement, where each hand in turn has to play two parts, often underestimates the significance of the sustained tones. He should, therefore, be urged to exercise strict self-control in holding down all sustained notes, and to this end a careful observance of the correct fingering is a prime requisite. For instance, take care not to play the measure marked above something like this: 𝄞 for then it would sound like a passage in one part. A real "Bach-player" must learn to play two parts together with one hand in different degrees of strength.

87840

(4) Notice the stretto (overlapping of the theme) in soprano and bass.

(5) From here onward a general crescendo should be developed up to the final chord, while always making the continually repeated theme stand out plastically.

(6) Stretto in contrary motion between alto and bass.

N.B. The outlines of the form of this piece are so vaguely marked that an attempt to indicate their limits by bars would be a rather presumptuous undertaking. It would seem preferable to consider this homogeneous, onsurging movement in the light of an introductory prelude to the Cycle coming after. The one-measure theme with its characteristic uprolling figure may be divided into two sections: either of which may be utilized independently, as occasion serves.

(**) In the first half of this Invention the thematic figure merely swells and subsides alternately while the modulation simply shifts from tonic to dominant; but, beginning with measure 12, a more and more animated upstriving of the movement is felt, which combines with the increasingly rich modulation to form a brilliant close.

87640

(1) In this and similar passages take care not to separate too sharply the two note-groups united under one slur, as one might be tempted to do by the repetition of the same note on the third and fourth eighth-note. Play nearly as indicated by the following notation:

(2) For the sake of distinctness, weak fingers may employ this facilitation:

A similar simplification may also be applied to the two trills later met with:

* As the decisive factor in determining the tempo we take the rolling sixteenth-note figure, which must not have a dragging effect. Similarly, the sixteenth-note triplets indicated by the editor meas. 7 and elsewhere should sound like a very rapid trill.

(3) Here one should try to let the added middle part (as mere harmonic padding) recede in force, and not to hold the five quarter-notes longer than is indicated; otherwise the F♯ (marked +) that crosses the upper part will unduly overpower the theme.

N. B. Where not the second of the two Sections (IA^1 and IA^2) which combine to form the First Part merely a faithful imitation of the first, and, of these two, the only one to close with a decided cadence, they might possibly be taken for two independent and distinct Parts. Per contra, the beginning of the Second Part proper is clearly marked by the development that does not start until IIA^1; to keep this development for a final Part would be an offense against the logic of esthetics as applied to formal construction. Furthermore, we cannot assume that the following Section IIA^2 is an independent Third Part, both because of its brevity, and because it recapitulates only the cadencing portion of IA^1; on the contrary, the basic form of this Invention is bipartite, though highly developed and ramified.

Allegretto
Briskly

3

(1) The half-measure ♪♪♪♪♪♪ is still part of the theme; it must be considered as such, for in the course of the piece this figure is regularly repeated with the theme, and at

(2) even has a short working-out.

(3) Through this interweaving of two parts the theme is distinctly audible:

The passage must be played in conformity with this conception.

N. B. The Editor thinks that the form, as here outlined by the slurs, is so indicated as to preserve both proportion and symmetry. The logical construction of this "fugued" passage is thus most clearly and convincingly set forth.

37640

(1) This bass passage (counter-subject) written in circles of fifths is deserving of attention because of its consistent repetition in the parallel and dominant keys, and should therefore be emphasized (though not too obtrusively) on each appearance.

(2) Here the middle part naturally comes to the fore. The two *e*'s (♪) in the left hand must be held down for their exact time-value; if held longer, the passage has the effect of a four-part movement, which, being wholly unwarranted, must be avoided.

(3) While strictly binding and noticeably emphasizing this chromatic counterpoint, the peculiar phrasing of the thematic figure in the highest part must be observed and distinctly brought out. This also applies (*mutatis mutandis*) to the symmetrical repetition of the same combination at the end of the piece. Considerable practice is needed for precisely carrying out this direction.

(4) The *a* held over in the lowest part has to be struck again, because it likewise belongs to the middle part carrying the theme, which would otherwise suffer interruption.

(5) What was said under (2) also applies here to a certain extent.

(6) The suspended second, *e*, must be carefully held down.

N. B. If this piece began, like a fugue, with only one part, and if the third part did not enter until the fourth measure, the effect would be that of a regular fughetta. In fact, the fugue-form, which is closely approximated in Nos. 9, 12, 13 and 14, is distinctly indicated here, so that from this point of view, as in general, the Bach Inventions are shown to be the most suitable preparation for the master's principal pianistic works. So, in this case, the three Parts night be described as the "Exposition," the "Development," and the "Coda," of this fugal movement. If you add in imagination a four-measure organ-point on *D* to the Coda — something like a fourth organ-pedal part — the fugue-character stands out still more strongly. — Besides, the Second (development) Section may be divided into two parts, the first entering in the parallel key, the dominant key.

5

Andante espressivo ♪=*
Slow and expressively

(1) The interval of a second in the mordent and inverted mordent is always derived from the scale to which the harmony, on which the melodic phrase is founded, belongs. The step of a second down from the raised seventh (𝄽) must conform to the ascending melodic scale; whereas the step of a second up from the lowered sixth (𝄽) conforms to the descending melodic scale:

C minor

* When beginning practice it is advisable to play in still slower tempo, and to count each sixteenth.

(2) In the original this is merely marked: ![notation] . The Editor has written out the passage in con-

formity with the preceding parallel passage in C minor.

37640

(3) In this one place the mordent is not inverted, thus lending new melodic charm to the descending close.

N. B. The need for writing out the graces in full was more urgent than ever in this piece, where the multiplicity of embellishments often causes the student to lose track entirely of the correct subdivisions of the tempo. Moreover, **they** are given, in the (probably) most popular edition, only in mutilated and abbreviated form, so that many of those in the present edition, being true to the original, may well give this Invention the effect of a new piece.

While carefully avoiding all sentimentality, the interpretation of this "duet with lute-accompaniment," with its well-nigh romantic atmosphere, requires most expressive execution, making great demands on plasticity of touch and variety in nuance. Even a moderate use of the pedal seems not inadmissible here, by way of exception; just to what extent and in what manner it may be used, is indicated by the Editor in the opening measures.

From a pedagogic standpoint, this composition presents itself as a useful study in rhythm and interpretation.

(1) While strict attention should be paid, throughout the piece, to holding down the dotted notes, this is not feasible in the two places marked by contradictory notation in parentheses.

(2) This chord-figuration, so distinctive of the Gigue-type, should not sound too *legato* (by reason of its leaping progression), and, although it progresses through three parts in alternation, it should retain a "one-part" contrapuntal character so far as possible.

(3) Here the interval-relation of the lowest part to the middle part does not admit of the "thematic" close

in the bass figure, which may be added mentally as follows:

(4) Beginning of a short development in contrary motion.

———————

* Only for hands that can stretch it.

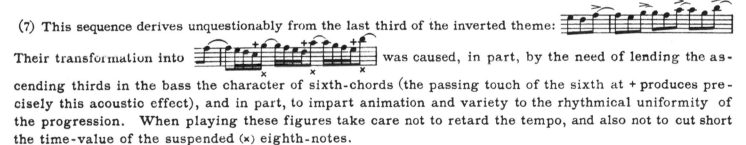

(5) Play the hold thus:  A hold on the chord of the second with the seventh in bass, near the close of a piece, is often met with in Bach. Similarly, Beethoven was wont to interpose a few adagio measures before the stormy final cadence of his impassioned compositions; a holding-back of the emotional urge which, when set free, breaks out all the more violently.

(6) Roughnesses caused by the clash of two parts in contrary progression do not distress the contrapuntally trained ear, which senses only the independently *melodic* (here *thematic*, also) significance of each.

(7) This sequence derives unquestionably from the last third of the inverted theme: Their transformation into was caused, in part, by the need of lending the ascending thirds in the bass the character of sixth-chords (the passing touch of the sixth at + produces precisely this acoustic effect), and in part, to impart animation and variety to the rhythmical uniformity of the progression. When playing these figures take care not to retard the tempo, and also not to cut short the time-value of the suspended (×) eighth-notes.

(8) If this figure is conceived as derived from the chord-figuration at (2), its seemingly illogical appearance will not cause surprise:

(9) The rhythmic energy of this resolution harmonizes ill with the melodically tame close of the dominant seventh falling on the third. Perhaps a slowing-down of the movement, starting on the seventh eighth-note, (taking each eighth-note in the time of three before), would serve to obviate this contrast; however, the Editor does not claim that this suggestion is above criticism.

N. B. The two-section form adopted here may be considered perfect, and a model for imitation, in so far as its proportions conform to those esthetic laws of symmetry according to which the larger part should surpass the lesser in extent by as much as both parts taken together surpass the first as regards extension. Of the sum total of 41 measures, the first and second parts have respectively 17 and 24 measures. This comparison shows a slight disproportion in the second part, which is equalized by the two *fermate.*

Andante con moto
Expressive, easy-flowing*

(1) The sixteenth-note figure arises from the inversion of the theme: and does not appear until

(2) in its original shape; its thematic significance explains and justifies the somewhat pretentious rôle assigned to it.

---

* The "expression" must not be exaggerated at the continuously flowing figuration. Here, as in all other of Bach's slow movements, be careful not to degenerate into sentimentality. The emotional character of the piece must be vigorous and virile throughout.

(3) Do not fail to emphasize the fine harmonic transition from *G* minor to *F* minor; it hinges chiefly on the clever enharmonic change of *e♭* into *d♯*.

(4) This short two-part stretto should stand out in strong relief; furthermore, the strongly contrasted contrary motion of the parts in these two measures should be enhanced by a *crescendo* and *accelerando* reaching its peak at the hold which the Editor thinks it advisable to place on the seventh-chord. — — The measure marked *quasi Recit.* ought to be "declaimed" freely and dramatically; whereas the *a tempo* following may be played a trifle broader than the original tempo.

(5) The thematic relation to [music notation] will be readily seen.

N. B. The second section, divided into two nearly equal halves, appears as long as the first and third sections taken together. Picture to yourself the architectonic idea of the relation of a central structure to the wings on either side, in order to banish all doubt as to the complete justification of the analogous musical form here presented.

Allegretto vivace
Light and cheery

8

mf
non troppo legato
p

ten.

marc.

p

f
p

cresc.

più cresc.

marc.

* The mordents (𝄿) are to be played throughout in the manner already explained.

** Here begins, together with the First Section, a chain of stretti continuing through three full measures.

* Although here, and for the first time, we lose sight of the theme, it sounds out distinctly in this second-part close; much as the light folds of a garment betray the outlines of the form it covers.

** Note the perfectly symmetrical relation of the close of this part to that of the first part.

87640

Largo espressivo
With grave dignity

This number — a piece of genuine "Passion-Music," and perhaps the most important one in the collection with respect to content — exemplifies, in its treatment of three-part counterpoint, a plastic clarity of form united to a depth of feeling which make this Invention a model of its class. Each of the three coordinate themes, alternating and uniting in contrasting effect, has therefore equal right to special emphasis in the proper place. But, as an endeavor to emphasize all the parts equally might easily result in an aimless overpowering of one by another, it is advisable to employ a certain "diplomatic" procedure, for which the Editor suggests the following fairly adequate rules.

Do not pay too much attention to emphasizing the soprano, whose effect is always the most penetrating because of its position; likewise the theme marked III, whether occurring in tenor or in bass, will always be distinctly heard by reason of its striking rhythmic configuration. Hence, only the third theme (I) calls for special accentuation, while the other two require stress only on their characteristic features. For instance, in measure 3 and 4 the middle part has to be brought out clearly, whereas in the soprano only the *sforzato* on the highest c should be specially marked.

But where theme III appears in the highest part (which happens only twice in the whole piece), and the player faces the problem of plastically contrasting the two lower parts with the left hand, he can solve it only by practising as recommended in No. 1, Note 8, for which this present Invention affords ample opportunity. — In form it closely approximates the Fugue, divisible into three Sections; the First comprises the so-called Exposition, through which themes I and II take their way alternately in all the parts, the modulatory succession being Tonic — Dominant — Tonic. The Second Section, obviously closing with the cadence in the dominant key, opens with a two-measure Episode modulating into *Ab* major, in which key the three themes enter first, then going over to its dominant. A further Episode of three measures, with imitation based on fragments of themes I and II, finally leads into *C* minor. — The Third Section repeats the Second in the key of the subdominant, the involved modulation into *Db* being carried out by the first Episode, lengthened into four measures. — For the final establishment of the original tonic, the Third Section receives an addendum in the shape of a three-measure Coda.

---

* In order to lend the close suitable dignity and solemnity, the Editor likes to double the bass "organ-fashion" in the lower octave, as shown below:

** One might proceed similarly in measures 29 – 31, in order to give full expression and energy to the passionate intensification:

(1) This sequence-like enchainment of the second half of the theme appears one in each of the three sections, alternately in the lowest, the highest, and the middle part.

(2) After long practice with all conceivable fingerings, the one given seems most suitable.

(3) The note falling on the first sixteenth of the third quarter, and tied over in the bass, must be restruck by the left hand in the next three measures, otherwise a break will be heard in the middle part. The same applies to the right hand at +.

N. B. Apart from the more distinctly moulded form, the character and pianistic technique of this piece exhibit features akin to No. 1 of the three-part Inventions. The suggestions for the interpretation of the latter are applicable in the present case. — Be particularly careful to play the middle part, which is often divided by the alternation of the hands, smoothly and flowingly.

87640

Andantino con moto
Fairly fast, with rhythmical accent

11

f ma non troppo

* FP, fore-phrase; AP, after-phrase.
** Where no slur is marked, play *non legato*.

37640

(1) The following four measures are to be considered as an internal extension of the movement. According to the original (ideal) conception the preceding measure is directly followed by the first measure of the After-phrase (AP):

(2) This measure forms both the close of the First Section and the beginning of the Second—a species of "elision" to which Hans von Bülow has already called attention in his commentary on the second movement of Beethoven's Sonata Op. 109. According to the Editor's conception, the two upper parts continue to hold out the close of the Second Section, the bass at the same time opening the Third Section with its ascending figure.

(3) The "extension" noted in the forephrase of Section II reappears here in similar style. By eliminating it, the connection between measure 9 of the movement and measure 1 of the Coda will be made clear:

(4) The Coda itself (which, except the two closing measures, is a strict repetition of the first fore-phrase) should be conceived as an added "Epilogue." This view is reinforced by an earlier edition (Hofmeister's), which reduces the eight-measure passage to three measures:

so that these three measures would then belong to the Third Section.

(5) In consideration of the preceding *ritenuto,* a retarding of the tempo should be avoided here.

N. B. In contrast to the numbers directly preceding and following, this Invention departs from the elsewhere prefered pattern of the Fugue; form and content of the piece remind one rather of a song of the ballad-type. E. g., the thematic figure can hardly claim the significance of an independent theme; it is properly a composide of the melodic, contrapuntal and rhythmical intertwining of the first eight-measure period, viewed as a whole.

As to its form, the piece is really a great chain of movements. The task of distinctly setting forth the mutual relation of the several links of this chain, was not an entirely simple one. After careful consideration, the Editor decided on the tabulation given below as most nearly fulfilling the requirements of perspicuity, logic, and proportion:

Section I	{	Forephrase =	8 meas.	(I = FP)	
	{	Afterphrase =	8 "	(= AP)	close in the parallel key.
Section II	{	Forephrase =	12 "	(II = FP)	
	{	Afterphrase = (7)	8 "	(= AP)	close in the dominant.
Section III	{	Forephrase = (11)	12 "	(III = FP)	
	{	Afterphrase =	17 "	(= AP)	Parallel with II = FP close in tonic.
Epilogue or Coda		=	8 "		Parallel with I = FP.

The precise, clean-cut execution demanded by the sharply-marked rhythm and knightly bearing of this composition must not—contrary to the general, conventional notion — be mitigated, for example, by the quick crescendo and decrescendo (———) of the tone so much in vogue. Only the two lyric passages already mentioned as "internal extensions" — see Notes (1) and (3) — permit and require, more especially in the treatment of the middle part, an energetic, rhapsodic, interpetation, yet without renouncing its characteristic virility.

(1) It is characteristic of the figure, which must be recognized as a part of the theme (see Note 1 to No. 3), that it *ascends* in progressing from tonic to dominant, and *descends* in going from dominant to tonic.

(2) Passages of this kind, formed by the sequence-like repetition of a thematic fragment, are variously met with in this collection.

(3) The procedure employed here (and occasionally in his three-part fugues) by Bach, of repeating the theme for a fourth time in the Expositon and in the dominant key, has very much the effect of a true four-part movement, and also finds its justification in the symmetry thus obtained.

(4a, 4b) Parallel passages at the close of the First and Second Sections.

(✧-✧) The somewhat extended Episode comprised between these two signs is to be conceived as a lengthy parenthesis, after which the movement is resumed where it was broken off, i.e., just before the parenthesis.— An (imaginary) linking of the two half-measures immediately preceding and following the parenthesis, will best illustrate this conception:

N.B. Concerning the formal structure of this piece, and also of the next number, consult the N.B. to Invention No. 4.

Andante
Quiet and serious

13

(1) The theme, which, with its threefold repetition, comprises four full measures in the Exposition, is sometimes compressed in the further course of the piece into three measures; the periods are then, however, regularly filled out by the addition of a fourth measure analogous to the original.

(2) According to the two extant autographs there are two versions of this passage: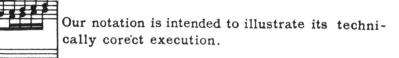

The Editor, in choosing the second, has modified the passage as printed above, in order to avoid the ill-sounding parallel fifths between tenor and soprano.

(3) In the original the measure appears thus: Our notation is intended to illustrate its technically core̓ct execution.

(4) Fourth appearance of the theme in counterpoint at the tenth and its inversions.

(5) Stretto between bass and tenor (lower and middle parts).

(6) The theme is heard clearly through these contrapuntal arabesques:

(7) The leading of the two upper parts apparently inticates their upward transposition by an octave; the close was probably conceived originally in the lower octave:

The cadence, however gains in brilliance and decision by this sudden upward leap.

N. B. For further suggestions compare the N. B.'s to Inventions 4 and 12.

Moderato
Moderately fast, clearly phrased

14

(1) The chord-figure of the countersubject, in its two forms: plays an important rôle throughout, which must be taken account of in the interpretation.

(2) Here the bass passage is to be regarded as the simplified thematic figure: whose transformation is justified and explained by the fact that the Coda entirely detaches itself from all thematic relations. This procedure is often utilized at the end of complicated contrapuntal movements for the sake of refreshing contrast, and likewise to indicate that the artistic resources are, so to speak, exhausted.

N.B. In the Editor's opinion this piece is the most fully developed one in the collection, and therefore— from the Bach-player's standpoint— the most difficult technically. The plastic accentuation of the stretti in the Third Section, avoiding every form of roughness and always maintaining an equable tranquillity alone demands no inconsiderable degree of artistic maturity. Hence, when this task is satisfactorily achieved, the student is ready to begin the study of "The Well-tempered Clavichord;" some of the less exacting numbers in this important work (e. g., the Fugues in *E* minor and *F* major in Book I) will very likely offer no serious difficulties.

The form of this piece, which closely approximates the fugue-form, is naturally exhibited in the following divisions:

> Section I = Exposition and Episode = 6 (4+2) measures
> Section II = First Development (mostly modulatory) = 5 measures
> Section III = Second Development (mostly contrapuntal) = 10 measures
> Coda = 3 measures

(1) All these dotted eighth-notes must be held for their full time-value.

---

* In establishing the tempo (which ought to be taken at a rather lively rate), the third measure, and those similarly constructed, set the pace. The thirty-second-note figure should therefore neither drag rhythmically nor, on the other hand, have too much of a bravura effect.

** "9⁄16" — that is, a tripartite measure in triplet movement.

(2) By this presentation of the next three measures the Editor hopes that he has found such an adequate compromise as will ensure the smooth execution of this some- what awkward passage. A still simpler notation in the third measure would be: but then the feeling of contrary motion would be lost.

(3) The tone of the sustained *e* will hardly be strong enough to furnish the chord of the second under the hold with a full-sounding bass; the necessary duration of this hold through another measure can be effected only by striking the lower *e* in the manner shown; by so doing, the whole preceding passage in *B* minor attains the satisfactory proportionate length of eight measures.

(4) A peculiarity of this close is the dotted half-note representing a time-value of one and one-third measure. By observing the hold, the six sixteeth-notes needed to complete the two measures are au- tomatically added:

N.B. The seven-measure section beginning here is to be regarded as a sort of interpolated Cadenza which (as such) determines the character of the whole piece, whose stiff figuration reminds in a way of old-fash- ioned organ-virtuosity. Certainly, the omission of the said seven measures, thus passing over directly to the measures following the hold, would make for more perfect organic unity and a more harmonious relation in the proportion of the two parts by whose combination the form of this Invention is fixed. All this goes to show that this closing number is not, on the whole, to be taken too seriously; it should rather be conceived as a pleasingly improvised "Postlude," a pendant, as it were, of the more serious sister-piece wherewith the collection is launched. — The interpretation should, above all, be entirely free from "modern elegance," to which the oft-repeated "jagged" chord-figure, and the somewhat easy-going jog-trot of the contrapuntal portions, might seem to furnish a temptation.